THE NORTH POLE GNOMES

BY DAN RAMIREZ

SPECIAL THANKS TO GARY, CARTER, JON, & AUNTIE J!

COPYRIGHT 2020 © NORTH POLE LETTERS
ALL RIGHTS RESERVED

FIRST EDITION, 2020
10 9 8 7 6 5 4 3 2 1

WWW.THENORTHPOLEGNOMES.COM

ISBN 978-1-7342453-0-1

THIS BOOK BELONGS TO:

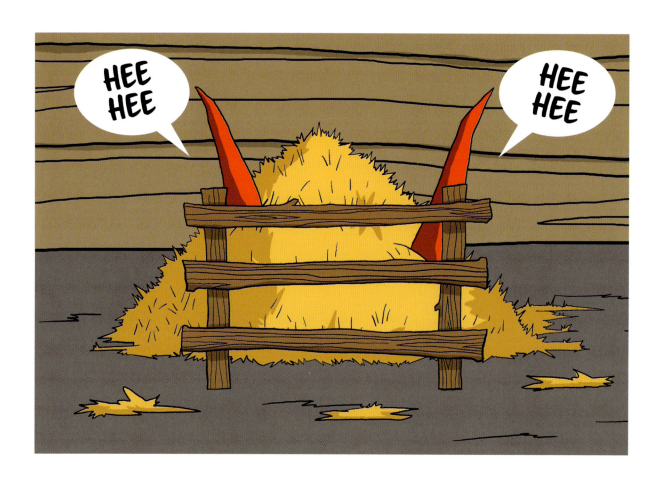

One day while Santa was checking his sleigh he heard laughter and giggling behind some hay.

Curious, Santa roamed the tidy stable halls
And found nothing but reindeer out of their stalls.

In the workshop elves were busy crafting toys
Who soon stopped to investigate a loud, loud noise.

The toys were dancing around in the air
But when they looked closer, no one was there!

So Santa and the elves came up with a plan;
"Let's solve this mischief mystery as fast as we can!"

And to their amazement, what indeed was so shocking
They discovered sleepy gnomes in every North Pole stocking.

Santa and the elves thought all night what to do
"Let's welcome the gnomes to join us - woo hoo!"

When morning arrived Santa knew what to say
To solve the shenanigans and make the gnomes stay...

"You may live with us forever at the north pole
But you must help me in an extra special role.

Elves make toys and reindeer fly...
I've got it! A perfect job you can try."

With a wink and a nod Santa said, "What job could be sweeter?"
Let the rascally gnomes watch my naughty meter!"

The elves held their breath waiting for a reply;
Then a gnome came forth, a smart little guy...

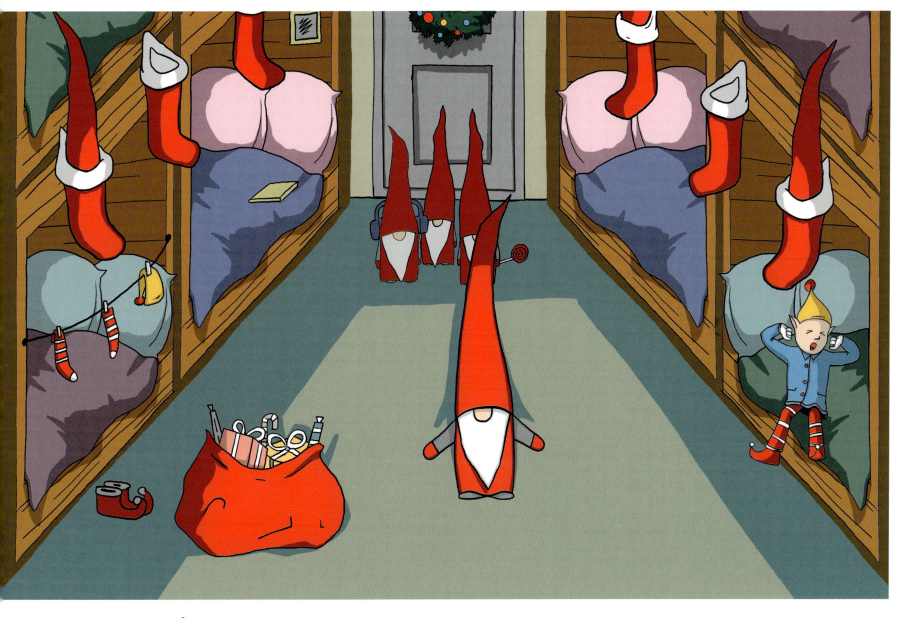

"We accept your offer but we don't want to roam;
May we sleep in your stockings and make them our home?"

Santa laughed and exclaimed, "Gnomes welcome to our crew!" and the elves cheered their new friendship steadfast and true.

So if you happen to see a North Pole Gnome
Doing prankful things inside your comfy home

HAVE A LAUGH AND RELAX; DON'T BE IN SHOCK
JUST MAKE SURE EACH EVENING THEY SLEEP IN YOUR SOCK.

Because while you're in your room, in your bed, fast asleep, the gnome returns to Santa for his duties he must keep.

For good girls and boys to Santa he will speak
But if you misbehave, the naughty meter he'll tweak.

The gnomes are free spirited and love to play
So be sure to have fun with yours each and every day.

And if there is mischief, don't worry or cry
Just clean up your mess...it's easy, just try!

For like the rascally gnomes whom Santa forgave
Your family and friends will too, if you sincerely behave.

Which is what truly makes a loving family home
Like Santa, the elves, reindeer, and the gnomes.

So that is how The North Pole Gnomes came to be playing tricks on Santa, the elves......you and me!